EXTREME MACHINES

PLANES

DAVID JEFFERIS

A+

Smart Apple Media

This book has been published in cooperation with Franklin Watts.

Created for Franklin Watts by Q2A Creative
Editor: Chester Fisher,
Designers: Sudakshina Basu, Ashita Murgai,
Picture Researcher: Jyoti Sethi

PICTURE CREDITS
Front cover: Stephen Fox, Back cover: Steve Flint
pp. 1 main (Riccardo Braccini-Aviopress),4-5 bottom (Gabriele Macri), 5 top (Library of Congress, LC-W861-35), 6–7 top (NASA), 6 middle (NASA), 7 bottom (NASA / Jim Ross), 8–9 top (Daniel Butcher), 9 bottom (Reuters), 10-11 bottom (Andreas Heilmann), 11 top (Bjorn van der Velpen), 12 top (Markus Herzig), 12 bottom (Riccardo Braccini-Aviopress), 13 middle (Yevgeny Pashnin), 14 right (NASA), 15 top (NASA), 15 middle (NASA), 16 bottom (U.S. Navy photo by Photographer's Mate 3rd Class Angel Roman-Otero), 16–17 top (Lockheed Martin Corporation), 18 middle (NASA/Nick Galante/PMRF), 19 right (Northrop Grumman), 20 top (NASA), 21 top (U.S. Air Force photo by Senior Airman Stacey Durnen), 21 bottom (Chad Thomas), 22 bottom (Ben Wang), 23 top (Steve Flint), 24 top (Northrop Grumman), 24 bottom (Northrop Grumman), 25 bottom (NASA/Jim Ross), 26 top (Courtesy of Scaled Composites, LLC), 26 bottom (Courtesy of Scaled Composites, LLC), 27 top (Courtesy of Scaled Composites, LLC), 28 top left (Library of Congress, LC-W861-35), 28 middle right (NASA), 29 middle left (U.S. Navy photo by Photographer's Mate 3rd Class Angel Roman-Otero), 29 top right (NASA).

Published in the United States by Smart Apple Media
2140 Howard Drive West, North Mankato, Minnesota 56003

Library of Congress Cataloging-in-Publication Data

Jefferis, David.
Planes / by David Jefferis.
p. cm. — (Extreme machines)
Includes index.
ISBN-13: 978-1-59920-042-2
1. Airplanes—Juvenile literature. I. Title.

TL547.J4424 2007
629.133'34—dc22   2006030842

9 8 7 6 5 4 3 2 1

CONTENTS

WEIRD WINGS

Mankind's experiments with powered flight began in the late 19th century, when many pioneers tried—and failed—to make a successful aircraft. Then in 1903, the Wright brothers made the first powered flight in their aircraft named the *Flyer*.

FLYING STEAMER

Before the Wright brothers flew into the history books, Frenchman Clement Ader had built a bat-winged plane called the *Éole*. It had a small steam engine and made a flight of just 165 feet (50 m). But the flight set no height records— most of it was only 8 inches (20 cm) above the ground! Even so, the 1890 flight was an important step in the history of flight.

THE WRIGHT FLYER

The Wright brothers became air enthusiasts after learning of other air pioneers. Their invention, the *Flyer*, was the world's first true aircraft—power came from a small home-built gasoline engine, and the plane was steered successfully throughout its many flights. To steer, the pilot pulled cables that actually bent the wings up or down. Today, separate controls called ailerons do this.

Pilot sat in small cabin

Éole

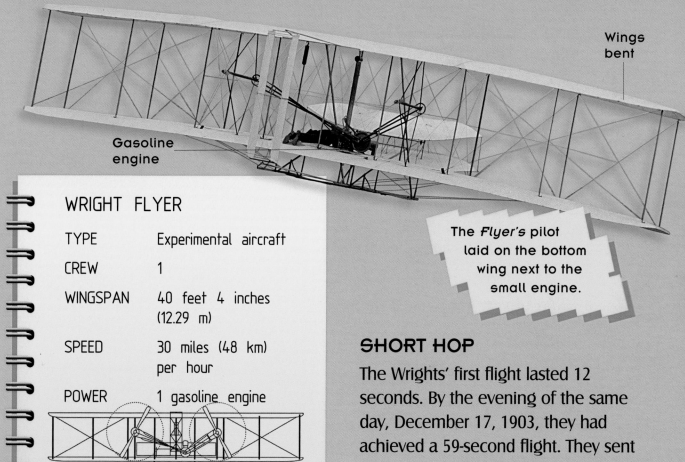

Wings bent

Gasoline engine

WRIGHT FLYER

TYPE	Experimental aircraft
CREW	1
WINGSPAN	40 feet 4 inches (12.29 m)
SPEED	30 miles (48 km) per hour
POWER	1 gasoline engine

The *Flyer's* pilot laid on the bottom wing next to the small engine.

SHORT HOP

The Wrights' first flight lasted 12 seconds. By the evening of the same day, December 17, 1903, they had achieved a 59-second flight. They sent messages to confirm their success, but many newspaper editors did not believe the news! Even so, the brothers had done it, and the air age had begun.

Éole did leave the ground, but had no proper steering controls.

Wood ribs kept canvas wings stretched

ADER ÉOLE

TYPE	Experimental aircraft
CREW	1
WINGSPAN	45 feet 11 inches (14 m)
SPEED	15 miles (24 km) per hour
POWER	1 steam engine

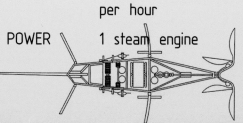

web

FINDER

http://www.flyingmachines.org/ader.html
Learn more about Clement Ader's experiments.
http://www.first-to-fly.com/
Visit this site for more information on the Wright brothers.

EXTREME MACHINES Planes

SPEED!

NASA

The X-43 looks like a dart! Its 12-foot-long (3.65 m) fuselage, or body, is covered with special materials to keep the insides cool during high-speed flight.

Since the dawn of powered flight in the early 20th century, many aircraft have been designed to reach top speeds. The first planes staggered through the air at only about 31 miles (50 km) per hour—today the record is nearly 150 times faster!

Rocket motor in rear fuselage

The Bell X-1 was shaped like a bullet.

Single-seat cabin

6063

FASTER THAN SOUND

In 1947, the Bell X-1 was the first plane to fly faster than the speed of sound—Mach 1 or 660 miles (1,062 km) per hour. This was a dangerous flight for American pilot Charles Yeager. Most planes at that time flew only a little more than half this speed.

BELL X-1

TYPE	Rocket-powered research plane
CREW	1
WINGSPAN	28 feet (8.53 m)
SPEED	670 miles (1,079 km) per hour; later versions flew faster
POWER	1 Reaction Motors rocket engine

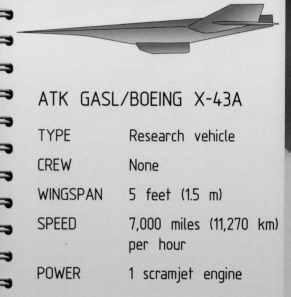

Scramjet engine under fuselage

ATK GASL/BOEING X-43A

TYPE	Research vehicle
CREW	None
WINGSPAN	5 feet (1.5 m)
SPEED	7,000 miles (11,270 km) per hour
POWER	1 scramjet engine

Scramjet engine under fuselage

A RECORD-BREAKING FLIGHT

In 2004, an American research plane called the X-43 flew at 7,000 miles (11,270 km) per hour. The X-43's experimental engine fired for just 10 seconds, but in that time, the tiny craft hurtled more than 13 miles (21 km) through the air! The record-breaking flight was made possible by a new type of engine called a "scramjet." This burns fuel in the airstream passing by, rather than inside the plane itself. Future scramjets promise even higher speeds.

A B-52 bomber carried the X-43 high into the air. Then it was dropped and boosted to high speed by a Pegasus rocket.

FINDER

http://www.nasm.si.edu/research/aero/aircraft/bellx1.htm
Check out this site for more information on the Bell X-1.

EXTREME MACHINES Planes

JETLINERS

One jet engine
under each
swept wing

Two-crew
flight deck

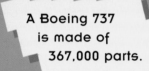

A Boeing 737
is made of
367,000 parts.

BOEING 737

TYPE	Short/medium-range jet
CREW	2 plus cabin crew
WINGSPAN	94 feet 9 inches (28.8 m)
SPEED	565 miles (908 km) per hour
POWER	2 turbofan engines

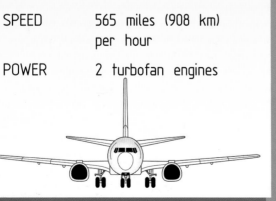

Until the 1960s, most airliners were propeller-powered and flew slowly. Today, all but the smallest passenger planes are powered by jet engines. Most are made by two companies, Boeing in the U.S. and Airbus in Europe.

A WORLD-BEATER

The Boeing 737 is by far the most popular jetliner in the world. Since the plane's first commercial flight in 1968, more than 5,300 have been built. Over the years, many versions have been made, all similar looking but with different engines or more passenger seating—early 737s seated about 110 passengers, newer ones can fit 189!

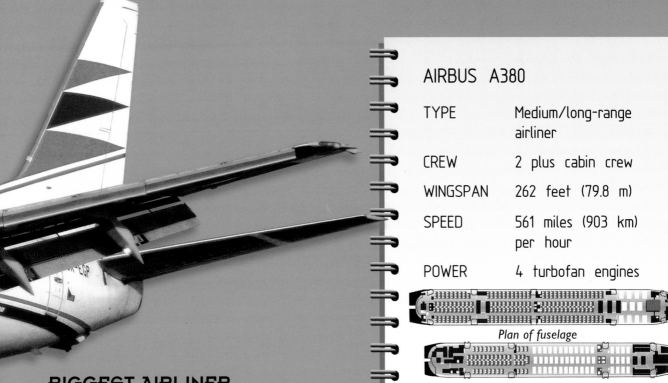

AIRBUS A380

TYPE	Medium/long-range airliner
CREW	2 plus cabin crew
WINGSPAN	262 feet (79.8 m)
SPEED	561 miles (903 km) per hour
POWER	4 turbofan engines

Plan of fuselage

BIGGEST AIRLINER

The Airbus A380 is the largest jetliner ever built, seating about 555 passengers in a two-deck fuselage—three, if you count the cargo deck under the passengers. Fully-loaded with passengers, cargo, and fuel, this air giant weighs up to 617 tons (560 t) at take-off and can fly up to 8,000 miles (12,880 km) without refueling.

FINDER

http://www.boeing.com/commercial/737family/flash.html
This is Boeing's site for its popular jetliner, the 737.
http://www.airbus.com/product/a380_backgrounder.asp
This is the Airbus site for the super-huge A380.

The Airbus A380 comes in airliner and freighter versions.

MEGALIFTERS

Most jetliners carry some cargo, usually stored under the passenger deck. Some airplanes, called megalifters are built to carry oversized loads.

FLYING WHALE

The weird-looking Airbus A600ST Beluga was named after a kind of whale. It's well-named because it looks like the animal. The A600ST was designed as a flying truck, up to 45 tons (41 t) of cargo can be loaded through a lift-up door at the front, while the crew's flight deck slots in underneath. For all its awkward appearance, the A600ST is an amazingly agile flyer—at air shows, the plane regularly flies tight turns at angles that make your jaw drop!

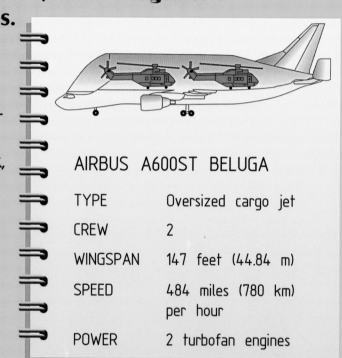

AIRBUS A600ST BELUGA

TYPE	Oversized cargo jet
CREW	2
WINGSPAN	147 feet (44.84 m)
SPEED	484 miles (780 km) per hour
POWER	2 turbofan engines

The A600ST's cargo door lifts up from the nose section.

Two jet engines

SIX-ENGINE ROCKET CARRIER

Russia's huge Antonov 225 was built in 1988 to carry the Buran, Russia's answer to the U.S. space shuttle. Instead of being carried in a cargo hold, Buran was carried on the An-225's back!

Three engines under each wing

Loaded with cargo, people, and fuel, the An-225 weighs up to 728 tons (660 t).

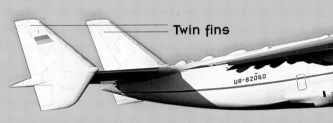

Twin fins

UR-82060

BIGGEST CARGO JET

The An-225 was not a brand-new design. In fact, the plane was based on another cargo jet that had two additional engines, a bigger wing, and twin fins at the tail. Only one An-225 was built, and it is still the biggest cargo jet ever flown.

AN-225

TYPE	Super-heavy cargo jet
CREW	6 and up to 70 passengers
WINGSPAN	290 feet (88.4 m)
SPEED	528 miles (850 km) per hour
POWER	6 turbofan engines

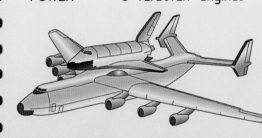

Cargo door

Flight deck below nose

web

FINDER

http://flug-revue.rotor.com/FRTypen/FRBeluga.htm
Many Beluga details are shown at this German aviation site.
http://www.air-and-space.com
Here you can see pictures of the An-225.

WATER WINGS

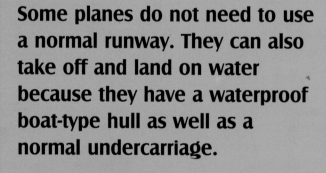

A CL-415 drops a water load that can be mixed with special foam to help put out a fire quickly.

CANADAIR CL-415

TYPE	Amphibious water-bomber
CREW	2 plus seats for 9
WINGSPAN	93 feet 11 inches (28.6 m)
SPEED	234 miles (376 km) per hour
POWER	2 turboprop engines

Some planes do not need to use a normal runway. They can also take off and land on water because they have a waterproof boat-type hull as well as a normal undercarriage.

WATER BOMBER

The Canadair CL-415 is the world's only firefighting plane that is amphibious, meaning that it can operate from land or water. The CL-415 is built in Canada where fires can rage in its vast forests in the summer. The plane can carry 1,352 gallons (6,137 L) at a time, and crews drop this load as a liquid "bomb" that can stop a fire in its tracks. If there is a lake nearby, the CL-415 does not have to return to base. Instead, it skims along the surface, scooping up a full load of water in just 12 seconds.

WORLD'S FASTEST

The Beriev A-40 patrol plane comes from Russia and is still the fastest and largest amphibious plane, even though it first flew back in 1986. It has two jet engines mounted high on the body to keep the air intakes well away from water spray. The A-40 was designed as a submarine-hunter. It can carry torpedoes and other weapons to drop on enemy subs.

The A-40 can also rescue people from crashed aircraft or sinking ships.

BERIEV A-40

TYPE	Amphibious patrol plane
CREW	2 and up to 6 others
WINGSPAN	135.5 feet (41.62 m)
SPEED	472 miles (760 km) per hour
POWER	2 turbofan engines

High-set "T" tail

Two jet engines above the hull

Swept wing

Like the A-40, the Beriev BE-12 Chaika [below] was designed as a submarine-hunter but has been adapted for firefighting.

web

FINDER

http://www.canadair.com/index.jsp
This is the home site of the company that makes the CL-415.
http://www.globalsecurity.org/military/world/russia/a-40.htm
Visit this site for some information on Russia's A-40.

X-PLANES

"X" stands for "experimental," and over the years many weird-looking planes have been built to test the frontiers of flight.

BACK-TO-FRONT WINGS

The X-29 first flew in 1984, and at first glance, it looked much like a normal jet fighter. Once it was in the air, however, the wings showed that it was anything but normal. They were swept sharply forward instead of pointing backwards. The X-29's designers thought the special wings would make it easier to maneuver in flight. They were right, but the wings were too difficult to make in large numbers. So far, the X-29 is the only one of its kind.

Single-seat cockpit

Jet air intake

Wings made of super-stiff carbon fiber material

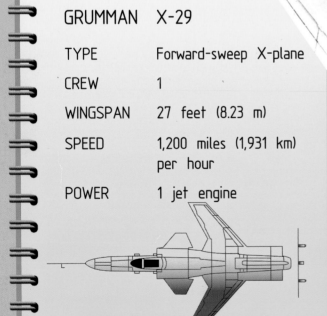

GRUMMAN X-29

TYPE	Forward-sweep X-plane
CREW	1
WINGSPAN	27 feet (8.23 m)
SPEED	1,200 miles (1,931 km) per hour
POWER	1 jet engine

Test pilot Chuck Sewell shows off the X-29's dramatic wing shape in flight.

The X-31 was flown for many years and some design features have been built into newer planes.

PADDLE POWER

The X-31 was another single-seater jet, but this jet had a triangular "delta" wing shape and an air intake underneath the pilot's seat. Its unusual feature was tucked away at the tail—a trio of ultra-tough metal paddles that dipped in and out of the jet engine's powerful exhaust gases.

As the paddles angled, the jet thrust from side to side, and the X-31 twisted, turned, and tumbled through the air. It flew at many air shows and thrilled crowds with its dramatic flights. It was probably the most agile plane ever flown.

ROCKWELL/DEUTSCHE AEROSPACE X-31

TYPE	High-agility X-plane
CREW	1
WINGSPAN	23 feet 8 inches (7.21 m)
SPEED	Mach 1.28+
POWER	1 turbofan engine

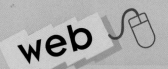

FINDER

www.nasaexplores.com/show2_articlea.php?id=03-065
This site gives an overview of early X-planes.
http://www.boeing.com/phantom/xplanesdt.html
Visit this site to learn about the latest X-planes.

JUMP JETS

The design of jump jets allows them to take off and land vertically, hover, and speed through the air. This is achieved by changing the direction of the engine thrust.

WORLDWIDE FIGHTER

The most successful jump jet is the Harrier. The exhaust from its jet engine is directed by four nozzles, two on each side of the aircraft. When the pilot pulls a lever, the nozzles can swivel to point down for take off and landing or point backward for speedy forward flight. The swiveling nozzles have made the Harrier an ultra-agile fighter that can beat much faster jets.

The Harrier has an unusual bicycle-style undercarriage. Most weapons are carried under the wings.

BAE SYSTEMS/ BOEING AV-8 HARRIER

TYPE	Jump-jet attack fighter
CREW	1 (2 for the trainer version)
WINGSPAN	47 feet 1 inch (9.25 m)
SPEED	661 miles (1,065 km) per hour
POWER	1 turbofan engine

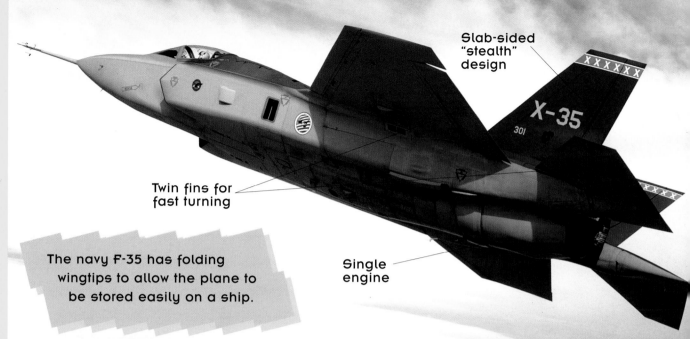

Slab-sided "stealth" design

Twin fins for fast turning

The navy F-35 has folding wingtips to allow the plane to be stored easily on a ship.

Single engine

AFTER THE HARRIER

The F-35 was designed to replace the Harrier and is a huge worldwide aircraft project. Present plans call for nearly 5,000 F-35s to be built. The basic design comes in three kinds—an air-force fighter, a navy fighter, and a special jump-jet version for the U.S. Marines and the British Royal Navy.

FASTER AND FASTER

The F-35 will be bigger and faster than the Harrier—but it should be safer to fly because its stealth design will make it difficult for enemy radar to spot. It's an expensive project though, likely to cost more than $200 billion.

LOCKHEED MARTIN F-35

TYPE	Strike fighter
CREW	1
WINGSPAN	36 feet (10.97 m)
SPEED	807+ miles (1,300+ km) per hour
POWER	1 turbofan engine

web

FINDER

http://www.airforce-technology.com/projects/fa2/
This site gives details of the latest version of the Harrier.
http://www.lowobservable.com/F-35.htm
Visit this site for information on the F-35.

FLYING WINGS

In a normal plane, people and cargo are carried in the tube-shaped body, or fuselage. Flying wings have no fuselage because everything is carried inside the wing itself.

ELECTRIC FLYER

The Helios flying wing was one of the most unusual aircraft built. Spanning an enormous 247 feet (75.3 m), Helios was propelled by at least 14 electric motors powered by solar panels covering the top of the huge wing.

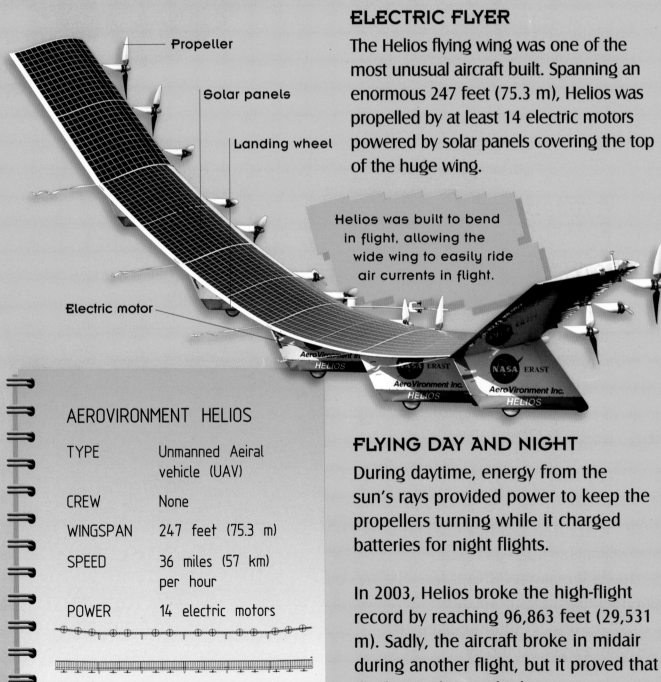

Propeller

Solar panels

Landing wheel

Electric motor

Helios was built to bend in flight, allowing the wide wing to easily ride air currents in flight.

AEROVIRONMENT HELIOS

TYPE	Unmanned Aeiral vehicle (UAV)
CREW	None
WINGSPAN	247 feet (75.3 m)
SPEED	36 miles (57 km) per hour
POWER	14 electric motors

FLYING DAY AND NIGHT

During daytime, energy from the sun's rays provided power to keep the propellers turning while it charged batteries for night flights.

In 2003, Helios broke the high-flight record by reaching 96,863 feet (29,531 m). Sadly, the aircraft broke in midair during another flight, but it proved that the basic idea worked.

PRICEY PLANE

The U.S. Air Force's B-2 bomber is the fastest and heaviest flying wing ever made. Fully loaded, it can weigh up to 187 tons (170 t). It is also the most expensive bomber ever, at more than $2 billion per aircraft.

Engines buried inside wing

Crew flight deck

NORTHROP-GRUMMAN B-2 SPIRIT

TYPE	Stealth bomber
CREW	2-3
WINGSPAN	172 feet (52.43 m)
SPEED	600 miles (1,000 km) per hour
POWER	Four F118 turbofan engines

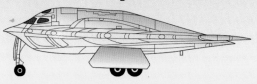

web

FINDER

http://www.is.northropgrumman.com/products/
usaf_products/b2/b2.html
Learn more about the B-2 bomber.
http://uav.wff.nasa.gov
Visit this NASA-sponsored site to discover other UAVs.

Northrop-Grumman B-2 Spirit's first flight was on July 17, 1989.

INVISIBLE PLANES

More than 40 years after its first flight, the SR-71 is still the speed record-holder for jets.

Military pilots need to avoid being spotted by enemies, and flying high and fast is one way to avoid detection. Another way is to fly a "stealth" plane that is built with special materials to make it difficult to see on radar screens.

MIGHTY BLACKBIRD

The amazing SR-71 Blackbird was built to fly very high and very fast. It first flew in December 1964 and still holds many height and speed records today. In 1974, the plane flew across the Atlantic Ocean from New York to London—3,471 miles (5,585 km)—in less than two hours!

LOCKHEED SR-71 BLACKBIRD

TYPE	High-speed spy plane
CREW	2
WINGSPAN	55 feet 7 inches (16.92 m)
SPEED	Mach 3.2; 2,112 miles (3,400 km) per hour
POWER	2 turbojet engines

STEALTHY SECRET

The weird-looking F-117 was the first combat plane to be purposely designed as a "stealth" jet. The strangely angled shape and special materials deflect and absorb enemy radar beams. Not surprisingly, the F-117 was kept secret for as long as possible. In fact, details were not revealed to the public until 1988—seven years after its first flight!

The F-117's pilot uses computer-controlled guidance systems to carry out an attack.

F-117 NIGHTHAWK

TYPE	Stealth ground-attack aircraft
CREW	1
WINGSPAN	43 feet 4 inches (13.2 m)
SPEED	646 miles (1,040 km) per hour
POWER	2 turbofan engines

web FINDER

http://www.f22fighter.com
This site tells the history of the SR-71 and also features many pictures.
http://www.sr-71.org/aircraft/f-117.htm
Find out more about the F-117 aircraft.

TOP GUNS

Top guns are the best pilots who fly the best fighter planes. The machines shown here are considered to be the deadliest aircraft in the sky.

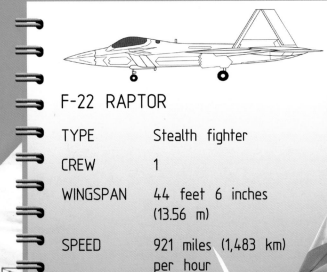

F-22 RAPTOR

TYPE	Stealth fighter
CREW	1
WINGSPAN	44 feet 6 inches (13.56 m)
SPEED	921 miles (1,483 km) per hour
POWER	2 turbofan engines

The F-22 is the most expensive fighter today at about $80 million per plane.

SUPERCRUISER

The F-22 Raptor was designed with one goal in mind—to be the deadliest plane in the air. Its two engines give more than 77,000 pounds (35 t) of thrust to shoot the plane straight up after take-off to more than 50,000 feet (15,000 m) high. In level flight, the F-22 can "supercruise," or fly at supersonic speed without any special engine boost, so it uses less fuel than other fighters.

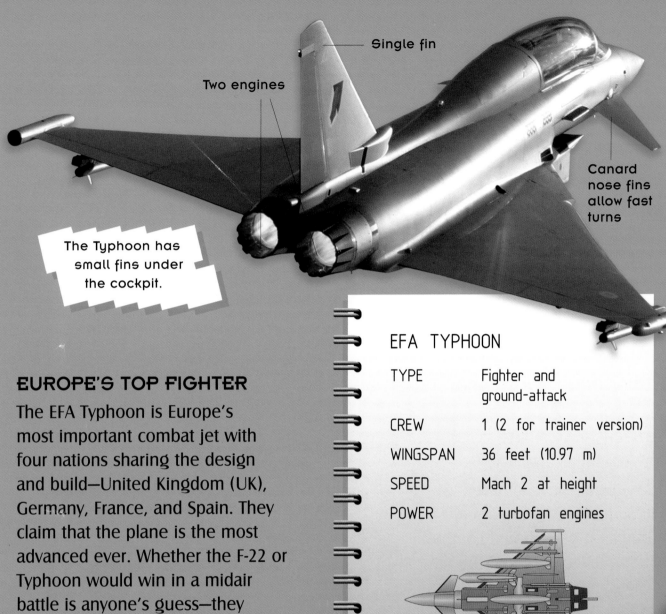

Single fin

Two engines

Canard nose fins allow fast turns

The Typhoon has small fins under the cockpit.

EUROPE'S TOP FIGHTER

The EFA Typhoon is Europe's most important combat jet with four nations sharing the design and build—United Kingdom (UK), Germany, France, and Spain. They claim that the plane is the most advanced ever. Whether the F-22 or Typhoon would win in a midair battle is anyone's guess—they haven't tried yet, although friendly test battles are likely in the future!

VOICE CONTROL

Among the Typhoon's many features is its voice-controlled technology—the on-board computers can react to up to 200 commands spoken by the pilot, making the plane much easier to fly. Like the F-22, the Typhoon can also supercruise.

EFA TYPHOON

TYPE	Fighter and ground-attack
CREW	1 (2 for trainer version)
WINGSPAN	36 feet (10.97 m)
SPEED	Mach 2 at height
POWER	2 turbofan engines

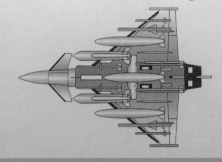

web

FINDER

http://www.f22fighter.com
This site about the F-22 fighter includes pictures and games.
http://www.eurofighter.com/Default.asp?Flash=True
This is the home site for the Typhoon.

ROBOT FLYERS

Satellite antenna under nose hump

V-shaped tail fins

Global Hawk has long, straight wings to help it cruise high above ground.

These planes are really "extreme"— they don't even have a pilot aboard!

HUGE MACHINE

The giant Global Hawk is a spy-plane with a difference— it almost flies itself, under the direction of on-board computers. The pilot-controller at the base changes height, direction, or speed using a joystick similar to ones used in computer games.

SATELLITE SIGNALS

Information to and from the Global Hawk is sent by a satellite orbiting in space far above. The plane can fly 65,000 feet (20,000 m) above a

target for about 22 hours, recording events below in daytime, at night, or even through thick clouds. Global Hawk's cameras can spot objects as small as 12 inches (30 cm) wide!

NORTHROP GRUMMAN GLOBAL HAWK

TYPE	Uncrewed spy plane
CREW	None
WINGSPAN	116 feet 2 inches (35.4 m)
SPEED	400 miles (644 km) per hour
POWER	1 turbofan engine

COMBAT ROBOT

The X-45 takes robotic flying another step forward—it is an experimental plane that can carry bombs or missiles to attack an enemy. Like the Global Hawk, on-board computers control the X-45's moment-to-moment flying, with changes in flight plan coming from pilots back at base.

PORTABLE PLANE

The X-45 robo-bombers are small, have no tail-fin, and the wings can be taken off in a few minutes for storage. When the wings are off, an X-45 can be packed inside a container. In the future, one transport jet could carry up to six robo-planes to a battle-zone airstrip.

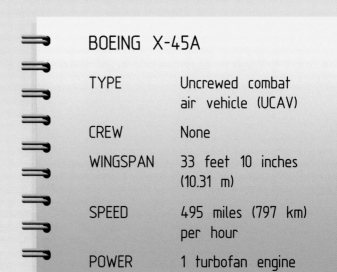

BOEING X-45A

TYPE	Uncrewed combat air vehicle (UCAV)
CREW	None
WINGSPAN	33 feet 10 inches (10.31 m)
SPEED	495 miles (797 km) per hour
POWER	1 turbofan engine

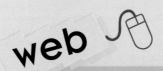

web

FINDER

http://www.boeing.com/defense-space/military/x-45/x45media.html
This link takes you to an X-45 site with pictures and videos.
http://www.is.northropgrumman.com/products/usaf_products/global_hawk/global_hawk.html
Visit this site for information on Global Hawk.

The experimental X-45 is the first jet-powered robot bomber.

No tail fin

Single engine inside fuselage

Wheels lowered for takeoff and landing

THE EDGE OF SPACE

SpaceShipOne carried underneath White Knight

White Knight's engines are there for carrying power, not speed. Its maximum speed is less than 185 miles (300 km) per hour.

SCALED COMPOSITES WHITE KNIGHT

TYPE	SpaceShipOne carrier plane
CREW	2
WINGSPAN	82 feet (24.99 m)
SPEED	185 miles (298 km) per hour
DROP SPEED	138 miles (222 km) per hour
POWER	2 jet engines

In 2004, a tiny rocket plane became the first privately built aircraft to reach the edge of space, more than 62 miles (100 km) above Earth.

BIG PRIZE

The Ansari X-Prize was an inspiration for space enthusiasts—$10 million to be won by the first private team to fly a craft safely to the edge of space, twice in two weeks. Radical aircraft designer Burt Rutan answered this challenge by creating the tiny SpaceShipOne three-seat craft to be carried by another Rutan design, the jet-powered White Knight carrier plane.

WEIRD WINGS

SpaceShipOne looks simple enough with a bullet-shaped body, seats for three, and a rocket motor at the back. Its unusual wings, invented by Rutan, made its amazing flight possible.

SpaceShipOne hit a speed of 2,250 miles (3,622 km) per hour on its up-and-down flights high above Earth.

CARRIER PLANE

The white jet carrier plane was the twin to Rutan's X-Prize design. Looking like some prehistoric bird of prey, White Knight carried SpaceShipOne under its belly for takeoff—climbing to a height of nearly 50,000 feet (15,000 m).

RETURN TO BASE

Once at drop height, White Knight released SpaceShipOne, then returned to base in a flight totaling about 90 minutes. Meanwhile, SpaceShipOne's pilot fired up the rocket motor and flew straight up, in a soaring arc. At the top, he released some M&M's® candies to float around the cockpit—after the rocket was turned off, everything in the craft became weightless for a few minutes!

SCALED COMPOSITES SPACESHIPONE

TYPE	Private rocket plane
CREW	1 (plus seats for 2 passengers)
WINGSPAN	16 feet 4 inches (4.98 m)
SPEED	2,250 miles per hour (3,622 km)
POWER	1 rocket motor

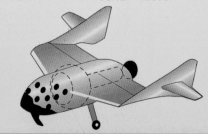

web

FINDER

http://www.scaled.com/
This link takes you to SpaceShipOne's maker, Scaled Composites.
http://www.xprize.org/
Visit this site for information on the Ansari X-Prize.

TIMELINE

1903

First successful powered flight by the Wright brothers in their aircraft, the *Flyer*, on December 17. The first flight, with Orville Wright at the controls, lasted just 12 seconds. By sunset, Orville and Wilbur had completed three more flights, with a longest time of 59 seconds.

1914

First airline starts operations on New Year's Day, using a two-seat Benoist flying boat. The plane flew 22 miles (35 km) from St. Petersburg to Tampa, Florida. The ticket for the 23-minute journey was $5, with an extra charge if you weighed more than 200 pounds (91 kg)! In all, 1,025 passengers used the airline, with only 22 canceled flights—a good record because early engines were unreliable.

1927

First nonstop flight across the Atlantic Ocean from New York to Paris. The pilot, Charles Lindbergh, flew alone on the 3,610-mile (5,810 km) trip. His plane was so extreme it didn't even include a windshield—the main fuel tank for the 33-hour flight was directly in front of the tiny cabin! To see out, Lindbergh used a mirror attached to the side of the plane.

1935

First flight of the 28-seat Douglas DC-3, the most successful airliner ever. The twin-engine prop-plane was produced in dozens of different versions; some even had skis fitted! Military versions were also made during World War II—in all, more than 13,000 DC-3s were built and some still fly today.

1939

First flight of Germany's Heinkel He 178, the first jet plane, on August 27. The world's first combat jet was also German, the twin-jet Messerschmitt Me 262, which was more than 100 miles (161 km) per hour faster than anything else in the air.

1947

First supersonic flight by Bell X-1 rocket plane *Glamorous Glennis*, with pilot Charles Yeager at the controls. The X-1 was the first of many X-planes—the latest one is the X-45 UCAV and further designs are in the planning stages.

1949

First flight of the de Havilland Comet 1, the world's first jetliner. It entered passenger service with the airline BOAC four years later. Sadly, a number of crashes forced a big redesign and rival Boeing 707 became the big jetliner success of the 1950s and 1960s.

1960

First flight of the British P1127 jump jet, developed from the "flying bedstead," a bizarre-looking machine used to test the engine. The P1127 became the Harrier combat jump jet, still flying today.

1969

First flight of the huge Boeing 747 jumbo jet, creating mass-market flying and the biggest jetliner made until the Airbus A380. A Boeing 747 had about 4.5 million separate parts, supplied by more than 1,500 companies around the world!

1991

First stealth aircraft flies. The F-117 Nighthawk was created with the help of radar research. It had special materials that soaked up some radar waves and sharp angles to deflect others. Most new combat planes have stealth features.

2004

First flight to the edge of space—62 miles (100 km)—by the SpaceShipOne private rocket plane. Designer Rutan is working on a bigger version for regular passenger flights.

1986

First around-the-world flight without refueling by Jeana Yeager and Dick Rutan in the odd-looking Voyager, designed by Dick's brother Burt, who also designed SpaceShipOne. In storms, the plane's long wings flexed up and down, giving a stomach-churning ride. Even so, the plane covered 25,012 miles (40,252 km) nonstop.

1967

The X-15A-2 rocket plane flies at 4,520 miles (7,274 km) per hour, still the record for a crewed rocket-plane flight. Like the X-1, the X-15 was flown to a great height by a carrier plane, then dropped in midair before firing its own rocket motor.

2005

First flight of the giant double-deck Airbus A380, the biggest jetliner in the world. Early A380s seat about 555 passengers, but bigger future versions may pack in 800 people or more.

GLOSSARY

AERODYNAMICS

The science or study of the forces acting on an aircraft in motion.

AFTERBURNER

A system that feeds raw fuel into a jet's hot exhaust, increasing thrust. It also increases fuel consumption.

AIRFRAME

The structure of a plane, divided into various parts such as the fuselage (body), wings, tail unit, and so on.

AMPHIBIOUS

A plane with wheels for runways and a sealed hull for use on water.

GASOLINE ENGINE

An engine that uses the power of gasoline to drive the pistons and a crankshaft. This turns the wheels or a propeller to move the vehicle forward.

JUMP JET

A plane that can take off and land vertically. Jump jets such as the Harrier almost always use STOVL, which stands for Short Take Off, Vertical Land. The aircraft takes off over a short distance, but lands vertically.

LIFT

The force acting on an aircraft that keeps it in the air. Wings create lift.

MACH NUMBER

An aircraft's speed divided by the speed of sound.

PROPELLER

In aircraft that are not jet-propelled, the assembly that spins around, creating thrust to drive the plane forward.

RADAR

A type of sensor that sends out radio waves to detect objects. Radar beams bounce off the object and some of this is returned to the radar equipment, which shows this on a video screen.

ROBOTIC

Any machine that controls itself to a great degree. UAVs and UCAVs are robotic because they are mostly under the control of on-board computers, with human operators giving orders rather than actually doing the flying.

SATELLITE

A spacecraft that circles, or "orbits," Earth, sending out information. Satellites are often used for navigation, broadcasting, or communications.

SCRAMJET

Experimental engine that burns fuel in the high-speed airflow, instead of inside the engine itself.

SENSOR

Any device that can sense objects around it, such as a microphone for sounds or a camera for vision.

SOLAR PANEL

Material that converts the energy from the sun into electricity; usually comes in very thin, flat panels.

STEALTH

Any plane designed from the outset to avoid detection by enemy radar. Stealth planes are built from materials that soak up radar energy. They are also shaped to deflect radar beams away.

STEAM ENGINE

An engine that uses steam created in a boiler to drive pistons to power a vehicle.

SUPERSONIC

Faster than the speed of sound, called Mach 1. At ground level, Mach 1 is about 762 miles (1,226 km) per hour. High in the sky it is about 660 miles (1,062 km) per hour. So, a high-flying plane traveling at Mach 1 is actually about 102 miles (164 km) slower than a plane doing Mach 1 near the ground.

TORPEDO

Pencil-shaped underwater missile used to attack enemy ships or submarines. Torpedoes are sometimes dropped from aircraft.

TURBOFAN ENGINE

Type of jet engine with a big fan in front to suck in air; uses much less fuel than the earlier and simpler engine, the turbojet.

TURBOJET ENGINE

A turbojet engine consists of a compressor that is driven by a shaft connected to a turbine, with a combustion chamber or chambers linking the two. As air is sucked into the engine, it is compressed. Then it is passed to the combustion chamber where the fuel is burned. This burning creates a powerful jet of hot gases, which propel the aircraft forward.

TURBOPROP ENGINE

A turboprop engine is an engine that uses a jet engine to turn a propeller. The hot jet gases spin the propeller, and this creates thrust to power the aircraft forward.

THRUST

The force produced by a spinning propeller or blasting jet engine that drives an aircraft forward.

INDEX